FSBO
7 Keys To Success

Rich Scott, MBA

Copyright © 2018 Rich Scott
All rights reserved.
ISBN:1725096269
ISBN-13 9781725096264

DISCLAIMER

Statements outlined in this book are simply opinion and thus are not guarantees or promises for actual performance. It should be clear to you that by law we make no guarantees that you will achieve any particular results from our ideas presented in this book, we offer no legal or financial advice

If your property is currently listed with a Realtor, please disregard this notice. It is not our intention to solicit the offerings of other Brokers.

CONTENTS

	Introduction	i
1	Do Your Research	1
2	Getting Started	5
3	Price Trumps Everything	9
4	Commission Is Unavoidable	14
5	Buyers Are Your Business	17
6	You Have A Contract Now What	20
7	Be Confident	17
8	Bonus Key	25
9	FSBO Is NOT For Me	27
10	Resources	30

INTRODUCTION

According to Investopedia, "For Sale By Owner" also known as FSBO, is a method of selling property without the use of an agent or broker. Generally, the reason that the seller does not use the services of an agent or broker is because they want to avoid paying a hefty commission for the transaction.

Did you know that you too can sell your home without a Realtor? According to the National Association of Realtors, statistically speaking on average 8% of homeowners successfully sell their home each year without using a real estate agent. In the following pages I will share tips and tricks of the trade to help YOU sell your home!

DO YOUR RESEARCH

There are many reasons a homeowner may choose to sell their home without using the professional services of a real estate agent and while you set the foundation it is important that you find your reason why:

- ➢ **Saving Money:** often the number one reason a homeowner chooses to sell their own home is to save on commission fees

- ➢ **Professionals:** Many professionals choose to sell their own home not only because it saves them money but because they have training and experience, Lawyers, Realtors and Real Estate Investors are examples

- ➢ **Less Expensive Home:** When a homeowner has a less expensive home they will sometimes choose to sell their home unassisted mobile homes, manufactured homes, condos and single-family homes in rural areas are examples of homes that may make sense to sell yourself

Once you come up with your "why" you need to weigh your options so you can be sure that selling your home yourself makes the most sense. Things you may want to consider are the cost vs savings, the amount of time required, your level of experience and your overall commitment to the work involved when selling without an agent.

Real Estate Agents have been around for over 100 years so to be honest if selling your home were simple more people would do it. Real Estate agents have stood the test of time but for sale by owners (FSBO's) have also had their own successes. According to the National Association of Realtors, FSBO's accounted for 8% of home sales in 2016, Zillow states that the number of successful FSBO's is near 11% so remember you have a real chance at success!

Savings vs Cost is something each individual homeowner should look at prior to deciding to list their home themselves. While commission may be avoided (not really, more on this later) some cost cannot. There will be a cost for marketing no matter who list the home. There may be additional cost such as the cost to list your home on the MLS or MLS like sites, to take professional photography and then there are contracts just to name a few. Many FSBO's choose to pay for the help of a Real Estate Lawyer to help navigate the process which can also create cost.

The amount of time that it takes to sell a home is almost impossible to express. In the chapter Buyers are Your Business, we will delve deeper into understanding what type of time commitment there is when selling a home. From showings to phone calls to random questions throughout the process, time commitment must be considered when deciding if for sale by owner is right for you.

Your level of experience in sells, marketing, negotiations, problem solving, attention to detail and customer service will come into play when you decide to sell your own home. While researching savings vs cost, vendors, and considering current and future time commitments also look at your level of experience in each of the above mentioned areas. Remember when you get your home under contract the likelihood that you will be dealing with a highly skilled expert in each of the areas is strong.

Much like time commitment, your overall commitment to the act of selling your home is something you want to be honest with yourself about, the earlier the better. The last thing you want to do is commit money, time and resources to a project that you can't complete. I only
bring this up because I have had the pleasure of working with multiple for sale by owners and most of them all started out with the idea that they could sell their own home only to realize they were not as committed as they thought. Remember only 8-11% of homeowners sell their home themselves.

There are many for sale by owner (FSBO) Web sites and services that have emerged over the years, with a quick google search you can find many additional resources readily available at your fingertips. Don't forget there is also a resource page at the end of this manual.

Only 8-11% of FSBO are successful so be honest with yourself

GETTING STARTED

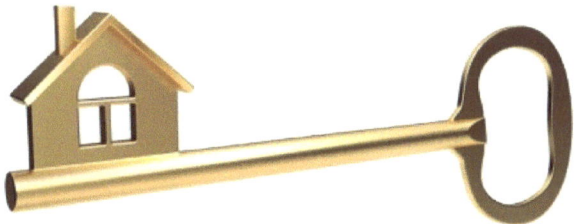

At this point you have at the very least verbally committed to selling your home! One of the hardest things to do is to get started, often times we sit around making great plans, figuring out all the details conducting research but we fail to take action and get started. When choosing to sell your home it is no different, you can get lost in the weeds very easily.

Now that you have completed your research and have a better understanding of the time and cost commitment of selling your home lets discuss getting started.

The very first thing you should do is get your home "show ready," this will include decluttering, fixing anything not working correctly and deep cleaning your home. While your home has been fine for you, buyers are going to open every door, look in every cabinet, open the refrigerator and even go in those areas you seldom enter.

If a potential buyer cannot see the value in your home because the wood floors are scratched and the windows are dirty your home is less likely to sell quickly or even at full price. When buyers are going through your home they will notice if the carpet hasn't been cleaned, each door that doesn't open properly, the room that is filled with too much furniture, each of these things make it hard for a buyer to picture themselves living in your home. When selling your home you want to remove what makes the home all about you and focus on making it inviting for buyers.

After cleaning and decluttering you will want to research properties that have sold near you, your goal is to figure out what the market is doing in YOUR neighborhood. It really doesn't matter what is happening 2 miles away as an appraiser will rarely look at properties outside of a half mile to a mile radius of your home.

Once you have a better understanding of what is going on and can answer what the market is doing near you, then you can decided how your home compares to those that have sold. Were the other homes updated more so than yours, did the other homes have newer stainless steel appliances, granite countertops, more bedrooms or a larger lot.

It's very important that you compare homes that are as similar to yours as possible.

After finding comparable homes you want to take the time to address any deficiencies you identified when comparing your home to homes that have sold in your neighborhood. A fresh coat of paint, new carpet or even a little mulch can go a long way in helping you get your home sold. Buyers want to purchase the house that is move-in ready and you are in competition with the nearby properties that are.

You know what's going on in your neighborhood, you've corrected deficiencies now it's time for the fun stuff! If you've never interviewed vendors well it's your lucky day. Prior to listing your home you want to have everything in place to move forward once you have an interested buyer so you will need to know who you want to work with in regards to title transfer and contracts so choose a Real Estate Attorney early (if you choose to use one).

I usually recommend three different venders to my clients. It's important that you research each potential vender you will be working with. If you use a title company remember they will be responsible for holding and distributing funds, so choose wisely. There have been cases where title companies have received funds and closed overnight. Ask for references and look up companies on the Better Business Bureau's website.

The easiest way to insure you are ready to sell your home is to do the majority of the leg work prior to putting your home on the market. There are three major things that happen once you place your home on the market, you conduct marketing of your home, go under contract with a buyer and finally you get to the closing table.

One way to compare homes is to attend open houses in your area

PRICE TRUMPS EVERYTHING

If you are under the impression that a home sells because you post a few pictures on the internet and place a sign out front you are sadly mistaken. There are three things that you must pay close attention too if you want to sell your home: Price, How Your Home Shows and Marketing.

PRICE

Pricing your home accurately is the most effective way to ensure a successful sale. No amount of marketing can sell an overpriced home. The biggest mistake that owners selling their homes without an agent make is under- or overpricing their property, the proper way to price your home is based on recent comparable sales. If you underprice your home any value in not using an agent may be lost however, if you over price it you could face even worse consequences.

When it comes to price many FSBO's will choose to utilize the Zesimate that they find on Zillow. It is important to know that according to Zillow their accuracy has a median error rate of 4.6%. While this may not seem like that big of an error rate, a home that is priced just 5% over market value will only appeal to 50% of potential buyers. Nationwide, Zestimates are currently within 5% of the final sale price 52.9% of the time. With Zestimates only right a little more than half of the time it is very important to use multiple sources when setting price.

Factors That Do Not Impact Your Home's Value:

- Original Price – what you paid for your house
- Desired/Needed Proceeds – the net cash proceeds you want or need
- Opinions – what friend s and neighbors say your home is worth

Remember that while you will determine your home's asking price, the buyer will determine the sales price based off of their perceived value. If you price your home too high, you'll price potential buyers out. Pricing your property at fair market value, from the start, will generate the most activity from real estate agents and home buyers. Your goal is to set the price so that you attract enough attention to result in showings and offers. Remember to high and you reduce potential buyers, to low and you give your property away.

HOW YOUR HOME SHOWS

It has never been truer that "you never get a second chance at a first impression" then when speaking about selling a home. If you can't get potential buyers to come to your home you are definitely not getting them through the front door.

How your home shows will play a huge part in how many potential buyers come to view your home in person. Photos are the first impression, and can generate interest and excitement, which leads to good offers. According to Redfin listings of homes with photos taken by professionals have about 61% more views than listings without. Listings without photos look suspicious and fail to give potential buyers reason to go see a home.

When preparing to sell your home consider hiring a professional photographer, but even before that remember to declutter, even a professional can't make clutter disappear. Photos taken with a camera phone may be cheaper but they are less likely to bring in buyers or real estate agents. A home is the biggest investment most people will ever make in their lifetime, so don't choose the cheapest route when selling.

MARKETING

One of the great evolutions in real estate over the last decade is the power of the Internet, and more than 90 percent of homebuyers begin their search there.

Since buyers normally start their home search online, it is imperative that for sale by owners get the exposure they need on numerous listing websites to reach their audience. There are multiple online sites that will allow you to list your home for a small fee, there are even a few that are no cost at all.

One important fact to remember is that when you choose to sell your home without an agent you are choosing to go up against the "big boys" and well the big boys have all the cool toys. As an example my clients homes are shown on up to 900+ websites, including the most-visited real estate websites in the world, putting them in front of potential buyers everywhere.

When you are ready to start marketing your home, write up a list of special selling points you think will attract buyers. Remember to highlight your selling points in your ads, and ALL marketing materials also don't forget to mention them when you're showing your home as well.

➢ Advertise online, put ads for your home on websites like Craigslist and Zillow

➢ Use Social Media sites like Facebook, Instagram or even Snapchat

➢ Rely on word of mouth, alert your friends, family and business associates that you're selling your home

90% of homebuyers begin their home search online

Rich Scott

COMMISSION IS UNAVOIDABLE

Most FSBO's decided to sell their home to avoid paying commissions, however most for sale by owners come to realize the importance of paying a buyer's agent commission.

According to For Sale By Owner, owners who pay 2%-3% commissions are 25% more likely to sell than those who offer nothing. Even if you choose to sell your own home you should consider paying some type of commission to the buyer's agent.

You may question why you would want to pay any commission but the reality is when you place your home on the market you are competing with every home on the market which includes homes represented by agents that are almost 100% likely to pay a buyers agents commission.

Remember that your goal is to get buyers in the door, many of which will bring their agent along with them. According to the National Association of Realtors, 87% of buyers purchased their home through a real estate agent or broker.

One key factor to remember is that a buyer's agent has fiduciary duties to their client the buyer NOT you. Ultimately when you pay a buyer's agent commission you are paying for the BUYER to have professional representation, which includes negotiating the price, inspection issues and any other real estate related concerns.

You always have the right to not pay any commission, however doing so can limit the number of buyers that view your home. Most real estate agents and buyers agree to a commission being paid prior to ever going to look at homes and it is customary that the sellers pay it. When a seller decides they are not paying a commission it leaves the buyer with the responsibility of not only financing their new dream home but paying the commission to the buyer's agent which can turn buyers off from evening looking at your home.

Be aware that most people who are looking at FSBO homes expect some sort of discount. They know there is no sellers agent commission involved, which creates more work and risk for them. Many will state this outright. This is a hurdle not easily overcome.

FSBO's that pay commissions are 25% more likely to sell

BUYERS ARE YOUR BUSINESS

Can you rush home from work every time someone wants to see your home? Can you excuse yourself from a meeting every time your phone rings with a potential buyer? At the end of a long work day, do you have the energy to take advantage of every possible opportunity to market your home? As a for sale by owner your answers to these questions NEED to be yes!

There are multiple hurdles you must overcome when you choose to sell your home, one of which is showing your home to potential buyers. Nothing makes a potential buyer more uncomfortable than the current owner being in the house. When a seller is present, most buyers will rush through a house and won't notice or remember much about what they saw. Try to keep this in mind when showing your home, try and be as non-intrusive as possible.

According to Merriam Webster a lookie loo is, a person who looks at something for sale without intending to buy it. As a FSBO you must be prepared to entertain "buyers" that are not really interested in purchasing your home. There will be tire kickers and time wasters. It's amazing how many people will set up an appointment and then never show, not everyone that shows interest in your home will be serious about purchasing

If you're going to be a FSBO seller, you must be willing to screen the buyers. Before you sign a contract with a buyer, make sure the purchaser will be able to come up with the money. The last thing you want to do is to take your home off the market to negotiate with someone who was never qualified for the home in the first place.

Selling your home is about exposure to the masses you must be available, very few people have a unique home. If buyers can't get information and access when they want it, then they just go on to the next home. You are now your home's agent; BE AVAILABLE!

Being available is not just being able to show your home but being able to answer calls, emails and text in a timely manner, ensure you think this piece through completely, How will you show your home while at work, will your spouse be ok with you receiving test and calls at all times of the day and night as potential buyers reach out? Do you intend on giving up your weekends after working all week to conduct open houses? Remember your job is to get buyers in the door. If you can only show your home on weekends and between the hours of 6 and 9 p.m., then you're going to miss a lot of potential buyers.

As stated in the 1st chapter Do Your Research, selling a home can be a real time commitment. You are responsible for all marketing, open houses and day to day showings so create a game plan early on to address each issue. Most FSBO sellers underestimate the amount of effort it takes to market their house. You need to keep the home clean, clutter-free and "show ready" at all times.

When showing your home always think about safety

YOU HAVE A CONTRACT, NOW WHAT?

If you have taken all the correct steps in regards to marketing your home, pricing it accurately and presenting it to the masses you should receive an offer. If you have an offer from a non-represented buyer understand that the buyer may have no experience with the process of buying a home. The fact is, that this is one of the many valuable services that a Realtor would normally provide, but now it is left to you, the seller, to walk them through getting to the closing table.

Every homeowner that list their home whether using an agent or not has one goal, to get to the closing table. To avoid issues, prior to accepting an offer, ask for a current mortgage preapproval letter from a reputable lender. It never hurts to give the lender a call to verify the buyer is fully qualified to purchase your home.

It is important to have a plan for negotiating and handling offers when an offer comes in you want to ensure you understand what it says. There may be dates and deadlines that you need to provide certain information by and missing them could void your contract or even cause you to lose the buyers earnest money if they walk.

Speaking of earnest money, get an earnest money deposit of no less than 1 percent of the contract price and deposit that money in your real estate attorney's or title company's escrow account. If your buyer breaks the deal without cause, then you may be able to keep the escrow as compensation for the time you lost on market. Earnest money deposits also ensure that your buyer is serious and committed to the deal.

Once you and the buyer agree on price and terms and sign the deal you are officially under contract, you can expect your home to be inspected once you pass this point This can be a tough point for FSBO's as it can bring up issues you didn't even know existed. Try to place yourself in the buyer's shoes and be solution-oriented. It will cost you time and money to start the listing process over, and the next buyer will probably have the same issues.

After getting through inspection things will often slow down until an appraisal is ordered, if you priced your home well you have nothing to worry about, however there is always the possibility that your home could come in undervalue. If it does expect the buyer to renegotiate the purchase price or walk away, no one wants to pay above a homes appraised value.

Once the negotiations are over and inspections and appraisals are completed, try to close the transaction as quickly as you can I would recommend speaking to your real estate attorney or title company as well as the buyers lender to set a date.

Place dates and deadlines on a calendar to stay on top of things

BE CONFIDENT

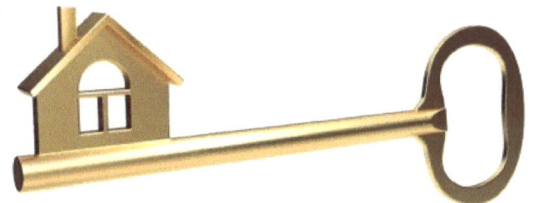

Selling your home is not an impossible task, however selling your home will likely be one of the biggest financial transactions of your life. Be confident that it IS possible to sell your home without an agent and save on commission. But also, be aware that it is a lot of work, takes time and it can be very frustrating. Before skipping a full-service agent, think hard about the time and effort you want to spend, particularly if the process drags on.

Zillow points out a very important fact **You're the neighborhood expert:** You can speak to potential buyers about not just the home itself, but what it's like to live in the community. After all, you know your neighborhood best. Sharing that knowledge can be a huge selling point with buyers.

Although you will more than likely be going up against a trained expert during negotiations try and pull on any past experiences you may have, just because you are selling your home yourself does not mean you have to give it away.

Prepare, prepare prepare. Did I say prepare? If you prepare for the sale of your home you will be more confident as the ball starts rolling. You do not want to be pressured to act quickly with no plan.

If you fail to plan then you plan to fail

BONUS KEY

There are multiple steps to completing a real estate transaction. Paperwork can be one of the hardest to get right, it is important to remember that forms can be based on Federal, State and Local laws.

If you fail to disclose a hazard, nuisance or defect and the buyer comes back to you after they've moved in and found a problem, they could sue you. Lead-based paint, seller disclosures and homeowner association documents are some of the forms that are required but often overlooked. Failing to provide certain documents can cost you the deal or even land you in court, to avoid these pitfalls consider hiring a real estate attorney.

FSBO IS NOT FOR ME

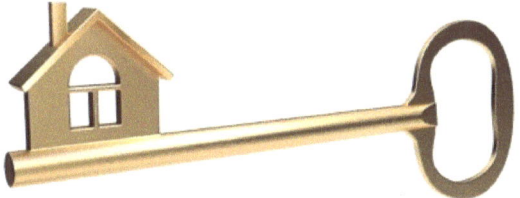

Many people that try going the FSBO route realize just how hard it is and eventually wind up listing with an agent. If after reading this book or maybe while trying to sell your home you have realized that FSBO is NOT for you I would love the opportunity to serve you. Below you will find a small snapshot of what I can provide as your Realtor.

Selling a home is not an easy task, however as a full time Realtor with years of experience my goal is always to make the transaction as easy as possible for you.

PRICE

In regards to pricing, in real estate, knowledge is power, and as your agent I am a local-market expert. By sharing current market data, trends and a comparative market analysis (CMA), I can help you make an informed decision about your home's market value and ideal asking price. Remember a home that is not priced right can end up sitting on the market and become stale and stigmatized by buyers. Once a property becomes stigmatized buyers will look to make offers below asking price at best or skip the property all together.

MARKETING YOUR HOME

When it comes to marketing I can honestly say no one does it better. We offer one of the most powerful and comprehensive marketing programs for attracting buyers and getting homes sold. In addition to our industry-leading online strategy, we use a proven combination of traditional and cutting-edge methods to showcase your home.

The largest number of potential buyers will view a newly listed home within the first 14 days on the market, and the number will decrease as the days on the market increases. Understanding this I have created a marketing strategy that keeps the marketing fire burning and the interest high on each of our listings.

Selling a home is a complicated process, but as your agent I will guide you through it every step of the way.

Give me a call
720-620-0498

RESOURCES

1. **Zillow.com:** Your home will be listed on Zillow and Trulia, Zillow is the leading real estate and rental marketplace dedicated to empowering consumers

    https://www.zillow.com/for-sale-by-owner/

2. **Owners.Com:** Owners.com has all the tools and resources for FSBO sellers. They also offer a free 30 day trial

    https://www.owners.com/FSBO

3. **Homebyowner.com:** Homesbyowner.com enables you to find and advertise homes for sale by owner in over 900 metro areas

    https://www.homesbyowner.com/nationalhome.asp

4. **ForSaleByOwner.com:** For Sale By Owner will help you quickly and easily create a professional-quality listing

    https://www.forsalebyowner.com

5. **Craigslist.org:** Craigslist is a free site and can provide a ton of additional exposure for your home.

    https://denver.craigslist.org

ABOUT THE AUTHOR

Rich, also known as the #BowTieBroker, takes great pride in helping his clients with all of their real estate needs.

Prior to becoming a Realtor, Rich dedicated over twenty years of his life to the United States Army, where he deployed to Egypt and Iraq in support of the Global War on Terrorism. While serving our great Country Rich found the time to earn a Master's in Business Administration to hone his professional communication and negotiating skills.

Rich understands that buying and selling real estate can be stressful. As a full-time Realtor, he works hard to lower your stress level and make your experience as pleasurable as possible.

To see what Rich is up to follow him on Facebook and Instagram
@RichScottRealtor

www.ingramcontent.com/pod-product-compliance
Lightning Source LLC
Chambersburg PA
CBHW040252220526
45473CB00001B/458